20 FUN FACTS ABOUT GRASSLAND HABITATS

FUN FACT FILE: HABITATS

BY ABBY BADACH DOYLE

Gareth Stevens
PUBLISHING

Please visit our website, www.garethstevens.com. For a free color catalog of all our high-quality books, call toll free 1-800-542-2595 or fax 1-877-542-2596.

Library of Congress Cataloging-in-Publication Data

Names: Doyle, Abby Badach, author.
Title: 20 fun facts about grassland habitats / Abby Badach Doyle.
Other titles: Twenty fun facts about grassland habitats
Description: New York : Gareth Stevens Publishing, 2022. | Series: Fun fact file: Habitats | Includes index.
Identifiers: LCCN 2020036347 | ISBN 9781538264478 (Library Binding) | ISBN 9781538264454 (Paperback) | ISBN 9781538264461 (6 pack) | ISBN 9781538264485 (eBook)
Subjects: LCSH: Grasslands–Juvenile literature. | Prairies–Juvenile literature. | Rangelands–Juvenile literature. | Savannas–Juvenile literature. | Steppes–Juvenile literature. | Illustrated children's books.
Classification: LCC GB571 .D69 2022 | DDC 577.4–dc23
LC record available at https://lccn.loc.gov/2020036347

First Edition

Published in 2022 by
Gareth Stevens Publishing
29 East 21st Street
New York, NY 10010

Copyright © 2022 Gareth Stevens Publishing

Designer: Michael Flynn
Editor: Kate Mikoley

Photo credits: Cover, p. 1 (main) Tom Bean/The Image Bank/Getty Images; file folder used throughout David Smart/Shutterstock.com; binder clip used throughout luckyraccoon/Shutterstock.com; wood grain background used throughout ARENA Creative/Shutterstock.com; p. 5 Kittiya/iStock/Getty Images; p. 6 shellgrit/iStock/Getty Images; p. 7 Kendra Koski/500px/Getty Images; p. 8 Jean-Philippe Tournut/Moment/Getty Images; p. 9 https://commons.wikimedia.org/wiki/Category:Eurasian_Steppe#/media/File:Eurasian_steppe_belt.jpg; p. 10 Dario Mitidieri/Getty Images; p. 11 ImagineGolf/E+/Getty Images; p. 12 Carl Young/EyeEm/Getty Images; p. 13 Helmut Hess/Moment Open/Getty Images; p. 14 Edwin Remsberg/The Image Bank/Getty Images; p. 15 Diana Robinson/500px Prime/Getty Images; p. 16 gabetcarlson/iStock/Getty Images; p. 17 Avalon_Studio_E+/Getty Images; pp. 18, 22 Danita Delimont/Gallo Images/Getty Images; p. 19 BanksPhotos/iStock/Getty Images; p. 20 Paul & Paveena Mckenzie/Oxford Scientific/Getty Images; p. 21 MOAimage/Moment/Getty Images; p. 23 DEA Picture Library/De Agostini Picture Library/Getty Images; p. 24 janetteasche/RooM/Getty Images; p. 25 Don White/E+/Getty Images; p. 26 David Fettes/Image Source/Getty Images; p. 27 Jeremy Woodhouse/DigitalVision/Getty Images; p. 29 Historical/Corbis Historical/Getty Images.

All rights reserved. No part of this book may be reproduced in any form without permission in writing from the publisher, except by a reviewer.

Printed in the United States of America

Some of the images in this book illustrate individuals who are models. The depictions do not imply actual situations or events.

CPSIA compliance information: Batch #CSGS22: For further information contact Gareth Stevens, New York, New York at 1-800-542-2595.

CONTENTS

Watching Grass Grow 4
Around the World 6
Great Big Grass 11
What's Growing On? 13
Farms and Fields 16
Wildfires! 18
Rain or Shine 20
Curious Creatures 22
Predators on the Prowl 26
Saving Grasslands 28
Glossary 30
For More Information 31
Index 32

Words in the glossary appear in **bold** type the first time they are used in the text.

WATCHING GRASS GROW

An old saying says doing something dull is like "watching grass grow." However, there's nothing boring about grasslands! You can find grasslands on almost every **continent**. But watch out—wildfires are common here!

These open, flat areas are known for—you guessed it—many types of grass. Wildflowers and other tender plants grow here too. All that **vegetation** makes a tasty meal for animals such as zebras or kangaroos. From curious creatures to wild weather, grasslands might be more exciting than you think!

If you visit a grassland, don't forget to bring sunscreen! Most grasslands have very few trees. That means there is little shade to guard against the bright sun.

AROUND THE WORLD

FUN FACT: 1

ANTARCTICA IS THE ONLY CONTINENT WITHOUT GRASSLANDS.

Grasslands are one of the world's most common **biomes**. In fact, they cover about one-fourth of the planet. Grasslands are usually found toward the middle of a continent rather than on the edges.

About 70 percent of Australia is grassland.

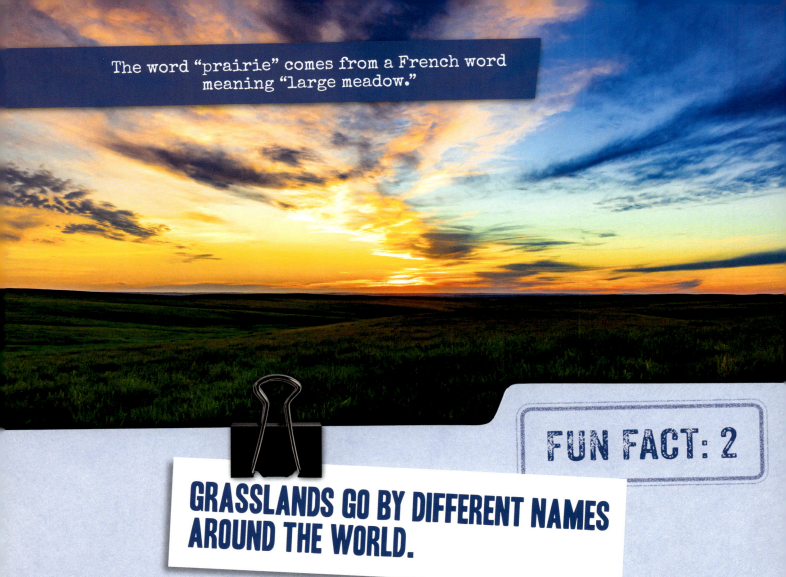

The word "prairie" comes from a French word meaning "large meadow."

FUN FACT: 2

GRASSLANDS GO BY DIFFERENT NAMES AROUND THE WORLD.

Grasslands may be called prairies in North America; rangelands in Australia; steppes in Asia and Europe; and savannas or veldts in Africa. South America's grasslands are called pampas, llanos, or cerrados.

The Eurasian Steppe is nearly one-fifth of the distance around the planet.

FUN FACT: 3

THE WORLD'S LARGEST GRASSLAND IS LONGER THAN THE DISTANCE FROM MAINE TO CALIFORNIA!

A trip between these two states is about 3,100 miles (4,989 km). The Eurasian Steppe is much longer. It stretches about 5,000 miles (8,047 km) from Hungary to China!

EURASIAN STEPPE

People have used the Eurasian Steppe as a trade route between Europe and Asia since 200 BCE.

A yak is a kind of ox that lives in parts of Asia and has long hair.

FUN FACT: 4

IN TIBET, NOMADS WANDER GRASSLANDS AND SLEEP IN TENTS MADE OF YAK HAIR!

A nomad is a person who moves from place to place. Tibetan nomads herd and live alongside hundreds of yaks. They use yaks for meat, milk, fuel, wool, and leather.

GREAT BIG GRASS

FUN FACT: 5

GRASSLANDS GROW FAR MORE KINDS OF GRASS THAN YOU CAN FIND IN YOUR YARD.

The more rain a grassland receives, the taller its grass can grow.

There are around 10,000 kinds of plants in the grass family. Grasslands are home to many of those, including buffalo grass, foxtail, purple needlegrass, and wild oats.

11

Shorter grasses in grasslands grow 8 to 10 inches (20.3 to 25.4 cm) tall, with roots about 3 feet (0.9 m) deep.

FUN FACT: 6

SOME GRASS GROWS TALLER THAN PRO BASKETBALL PLAYERS!

Lebron James is 6 feet, 9 inches (2.1 m) tall. The tallest kinds of grasses in grasslands can grow up to 9 feet (2.7 m) tall! Underground, their roots can stretch another 6 feet (1.8 m) long.

WHAT'S GROWING ON?

FUN FACT: 7

GRASS ISN'T THE ONLY THING THAT GROWS IN GRASSLANDS.

These biomes are packed with flower power. You can find a few hundred different kinds of flowers in grasslands, including coneflowers, sunflowers, asters, blazing stars, clover, wild indigo, and goldenrod.

Other plants, such as those in the pea family, milkweeds, and more, grow in grasslands too.

FUN FACT: 8

IF YOU'RE A TREE, A GRASSLAND IS THE LAST PLACE YOU WANT TO BE!

Trees and other woody plants, such as shrubs, usually don't survive long in grasslands. Why not? Plant-eating animals, wildfires, and dry weather keep them from growing too tall.

Grazing animals, such as these bison, like to snack on **tender young plants**.

An acacia's taproot, or main root, can grow as long as 115 feet (35 m) to reach water deep under the dry savanna.

FUN FACT: 9

THE ACACIA TREE SURVIVES THE AFRICAN SAVANNA WITH SURPRISING ADAPTATIONS, INCLUDING AN ARMY OF ANTS!

Animals that try to snack on this tree are in for a bad surprise. Stinging ants live inside the acacia's pointy thorns. Acacia bark is also fire **resistant**.

FARMS AND FIELDS

FUN FACT: 10

YOU'VE PROBABLY EATEN GRASS FROM THE GREAT PLAINS—AND LIKED IT!

Grains such as corn and wheat are part of the grass family. The Great Plains area is known for growing these and other crops because of its rich soil and long growing season.

The Great Plains area stretches from Texas in the South past Montana and North Dakota in the North all the way to Canada.

Today, people use much of the world's grasslands as space to plant crops, graze farm animals, or construct buildings.

FUN FACT: 11

GRASSLAND SOIL DOESN'T SLEEP, BUT IT CAN GET "TIRED"!

Grasslands make great farmland, but overuse can harm the earth. "Crop rotation" means to change what and where you plant. This keeps soil healthy and guards against pests too.

WILDFIRES!

FUN FACT: 12

GRASSLANDS NEED FIRE TO STAY HEALTHY!

Fire clears away loose brush, while plant buds survive underground. The warm soil wakes up tiny **microbes** to eat the dead brush. Microbes put **nutrients** back into the soil. This helps new plants grow!

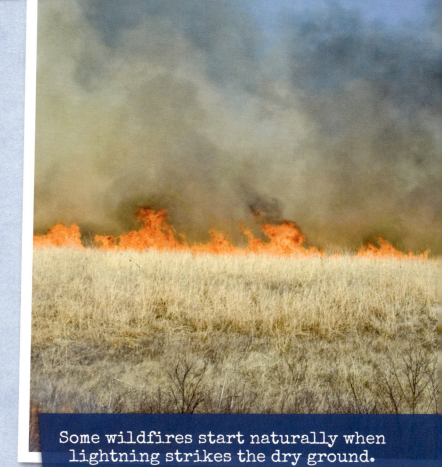

Some wildfires start naturally when lightning strikes the dry ground.

A "burn boss" is the lead firefighter who controls the burn and keeps everything safe.

FUN FACT: 13

A "BURN BOSS" LIGHTS GRASSLANDS ON FIRE ... ON PURPOSE!

Planned fires help create the right balance of **habitat** and food for birds, bugs, and other animals that live in grasslands. Skilled workers make sure the fire doesn't get out of control.

RAIN OR SHINE

FUN FACT: 14

GRASSLANDS ARE WETTER THAN DESERTS BUT DRIER THAN FORESTS.

Forests have plenty of rain to keep trees and plants alive. Deserts have very little rain and few plants. Grasslands are in the middle! In fact, they are often found between deserts and forests.

Most grasslands get between 10 and 40 inches (25.4 and 101.6 cm) of rain per year.

20

Tropical grasslands are mostly found in Africa and Australia. Temperate grasslands are found in North and South America, Europe, and Asia.

FUN FACT: 15

SCIENTISTS GROUP GRASSLANDS BY RAINFALL AND TEMPERATURE.

There are two main types of grasslands. Temperate, or mild, grasslands have warm summers and cold winters with less rain. Tropical, or hot, grasslands are warm all year with wet and dry seasons.

CURIOUS CREATURES

FUN FACT: 16

PRAIRIE DOG HOMES HAVE SEPARATE ROOMS, CALLED CHAMBERS, WHERE THEY EAT, SLEEP, AND USE THE BATHROOM!

These creatures build their homes 3 to 6 feet (0.9 to 1.8 m) underground in the Great Plains. One acre (0.4 ha) of grassland can have as many as 50 holes to enter!

Prairie dogs are part of the same family that squirrels belong to.

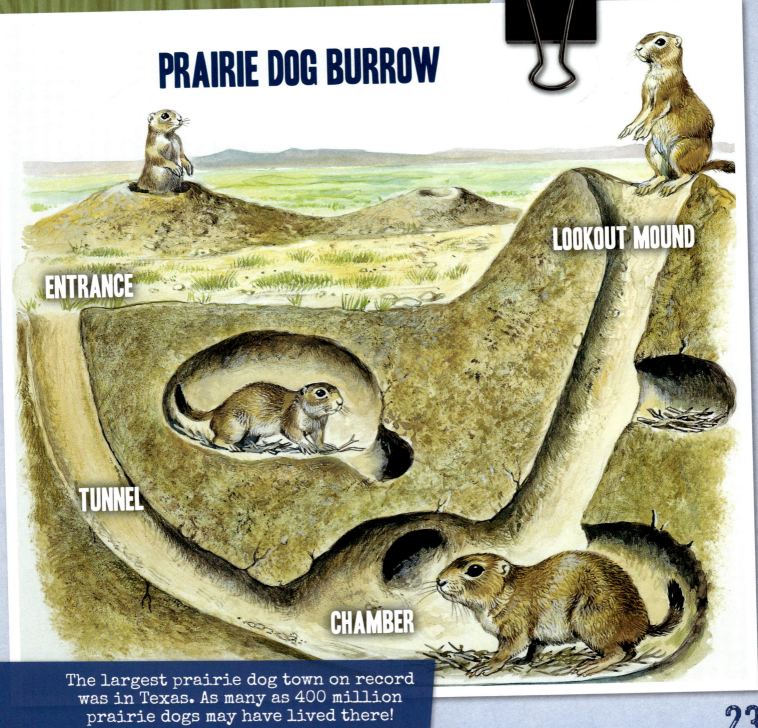

FUN FACT: 17

THE WORLD'S BIGGEST BIRD LIVES IN THE AFRICAN SAVANNA.

Even with their huge size, ostriches can run almost twice as fast as the world's fastest human! They can reach top speeds of 43 miles (69.2 km) per hour.

Ostriches can reach 9 feet (2.7 m) tall and weigh more than 280 pounds (127 kg).

Yellowstone National Park is a famous place where you can see bison in the wild.

FUN FACT: 18

BISON SPEND 9 TO 11 HOURS PER DAY SNACKING ON PLANTS!

Around 30 million bison used to roam North America's grasslands. By the late 1800s, European settlers had killed so many that only several hundred remained. **Conservation** efforts, such as those in national parks, brought bison back.

PREDATORS ON THE PROWL

FUN FACT: 19

WITH FEW PLACES TO HIDE IN GRASSLANDS, ANIMALS EVOLVED TO RUN FAST!

For grazing animals, living in a grassland can be great ... until a predator comes along! Many grazing animals evolved to have long, strong legs to help them escape.

Mammals with hooves, such as bison and antelope, are called ungulates (UHN-gyuh-letz). Living in herds protects them too.

Lions mostly hunt medium-sized animals such as zebras and antelope. It's not common, but lions also sometimes eat small elephants, giraffes, or hippopotamuses!

FUN FACT: 20

LIONS' FUR MATCHES THE GRASS SO THEY CAN SNEAK UP ON PREY.

Male lions stay back to guard their territory. Female lions do most of the hunting. They are very quiet and hunt at night to avoid being seen.

SAVING GRASSLANDS

The lack of water in grasslands makes them **fragile**. Too much human activity, such as farming and grazing, can harm plants, animals, and people. In the 1930s, a big drought hit the Great Plains. Black blizzards of dust blocked the sun and made people sick. This was called the Dust Bowl.

Fewer than 10 percent of the world's grasslands are protected. We can learn from our past to save these lands for the future. Which grassland would you like to visit someday?

In the 1930s, farmers dug up native grasses to plant crops. The Dust Bowl taught us what can happen if humans overwork the land without thinking of the effects.

GLOSSARY

adaptation: a change in a type of animal that makes it better able to live in its surroundings

biome: a natural community of plants and animals, such as a forest or desert

conservation: the care of the natural world

continent: one of Earth's seven great landmasses

evolve: to grow and change over time

fragile: easily breakable

graze: to eat grass or other plants that are growing in a field

habitat: the place or type of place where a plant or animal naturally or normally lives or grows

mammal: a warm-blooded animal that has a backbone and hair, breathes air, and feeds milk to its young

microbe: a very tiny living thing that can only be seen with a microscope

nutrient: something a living thing needs to grow and stay alive

resistant: not affected or harmed by something

vegetation: trees, bushes, and other plants

FOR MORE INFORMATION

BOOKS

Cocca, Lisa Colozza. *Grassland Animals.* North Mankato, MN: Rourke Educational Media, 2020.

Spilsbury, Louise and Richard Spilsbury. *Grassland Biomes.* New York, NY: Crabtree Publishing Company, 2018.

WEBSITES

American Prairie Reserve: Kid's Corner
www.americanprairie.org/kids-corner
Print coloring pages, word searches, and connect-the-dots games on this fun website for kids.

Grassland Habitat
kids.nationalgeographic.com/explore/nature/habitats/grassland/
Read fun facts and see a photo slideshow of grassland plants and animals.

Spectacular Savannas
kids.sandiegozoo.org/stories/spectacular-savannas
Watch animal videos and learn about African grasslands here.

Publisher's note to educators and parents: Our editors have carefully reviewed these websites to ensure that they are suitable for students. Many websites change frequently, however, and we cannot guarantee that a site's future contents will continue to meet our high standards of quality and educational value. Be advised that students should be closely supervised whenever they access the internet.

INDEX

acacia 15
Africa 7, 21
Antarctica 6
Asia 7, 9, 10, 21
Australia 6, 7, 21
biomes 6, 13
bison 14, 25, 26
"burn boss" 19
Canada 16
cerrados 7
China 8
corn 16
Dust Bowl 28, 29
Eurasian Steppe 8, 9
Europe 7, 9, 21
flowers 4, 13
grass 4, 11, 12, 13, 16
Great Plains 16, 22, 28
Hungary 8
lions 27
llanos 7
Montana 16
North America 7, 21, 25
North Dakota 16
ostriches 24
pampas 7
prairie dogs 22, 23
prairies 7
rain 11, 20, 21
rangelands 7
savannas 7, 15, 24
soil 16, 17, 18
South America 7, 21
steppes 7, 8, 9
temperate grasslands 21
Texas 16, 23
Tibet 10
trees 5, 14, 15, 20
tropical grasslands 21
veldts 7
weather 4, 14
wheat 16
wildfires 4, 14, 18
yaks 10